antoinette cooper

UNRULY

poems

Unruly

Published by Legacy Book Press, LLC.

Cover image © 2024 Theik Smith Photography

Author photo © 2024 Theik Smith Photography

Book cover design and interior formatting by 100 Covers.

ISBN: 979-8-9891170-7-9

Library of Congress Case No: 1-14447052383

"When we speak, we are afraid our words will not be heard or welcomed. But when we are silent, we are still afraid. So it is better to speak." - Audre Lorde

To our ancestors—known and unknown—we are listening

to your echoes about the ways your bodies said no,

and we offer love to the wounds.

CONTENTS

SENSITIVITY ACKNOWLEDGMENT

"Life for me ain't been no crystal stair."

UNRULY holds my stories, the stories of other Black women, and the echoes of some of our ancestral voices. In this collection, the tacks, splinters, and torn up boards Langston Hughes names in his poem "Mother to Son" are given language. While I have done my best to handle these narratives with care and respect, I recognize that some of the content may be activating for some readers, particularly those with the lived experience of trauma.

The structure of UNRULY mirrors the fragmented nature of trauma and memory, as well as the historical erasure of Black women's experiences. Gaps, repetitions, and abrupt transitions are not flaws, but integral parts of this narrative. This approach reflects the chaos often experienced in navigating trauma, illness, and systemic oppression. As you sit in ceremony with these poems, I invite you to befriend any discomfort that arises, recognizing it as part of the journey towards understanding and healing.

Please know that your well-being is also a priority. I encourage you to engage with this book at your own pace, to honor your boundaries and reactions, and to seek support if needed. You are the expert of your experience.

My intention in sharing these stories is not to speak for all survivors, but to create a space where some collective truths can be witnessed and honored. In amplifying these voices—both unique and universal—I hope to contribute to a larger conversation about the impact of trauma on our lives and the fierce resilience we embody.

In sharing our stories, we reclaim our voices, bodies, and right to take up space. We become the authors of our narrative, and in doing so, invite others to bring their whole selves to the page. If you see your experiences reflected in these pages, please know you are not alone. Both you and your stories are worthy of witness. If you do not see your experiences here, then may you honor the window that allows you to view stories different from your own.

If you or someone you know is in crisis, please reach out for help. Resources include:

1. Crisis Text Line: text HOME to 741741

2. National Alliance on Mental Illness (NAMI) Helpline: 1-800-950-NAMI (6264) or info@nami.org

3. RAINN (Rape, Abuse & Incest National Network): 1-800-656-HOPE (4673) or https://www.rainn.org

INTRODUCTION

Lying on the operating table, my abdomen etched with a new geography of pain, I knew my body was not my own. As the anesthesia wore off, I heard myself humming and felt the searing heat of metal piercing my skin. I had become a stranger to myself, a land where something ancient and unnameable had staked its claim. But this violation was not the first, nor would it be the last. My body had long been a site where others laid their claims, a battleground where I learned to survive.

Later, as I traced the scars on my belly, I found myself tracing a history of scars stretching back centuries—the scars left on the bodies of Black women by the legacy of medical experimentation, neglect, and abuse. Anarcha, Betsey, Lucy: the names of the mothers of modern gynecology, enslaved women whose pain paved the way for advances from which they would never benefit.

UNRULY is born from this lineage of wounds, a testament to the ways in which Black women's bodies have been rendered simultaneously invisible and hypervisible, disregarded, and dehumanized. Through a kaleidoscope of poetry, memoir, and documentary evidence, I map the terrains of my own body and the bodies of my foremothers, unearthing stories that have been buried in my DNA. These are the stories I almost took to the grave, the stories that demanded to be told, the stories that insisted on their own tongue.

In the fractured language of these poems, I bear witness to the pervasive assaults on our bodies and spirits: the everyday violences of racism, the intergenerational reverberations of trauma, and the wounds that fester beneath our skin and our collective unconscious. I trace the patterns of resilience, resistance, and refusal that repeat across scales, from the cellular to the social, the individual to the ancestral.

This book is also a reckoning with the realities of chronic illness, a burden that disproportionately affects women, with compounding risks for Black women. Through my own health journey, I came to understand the ways chronic illness was not merely a personal struggle, but a reflection of the deeper, systemic inequities that plague our society. Chronic illness demands a reimagining of our relationships to our bodies and our world—a recognition that healing is a continuous, communal process.

But even as this book grapples with the brutalities inflicted on Black women's bodies, it also dares to imagine a future beyond this legacy of pain. These poems become incantations, prayers for a world in which Black women's bodies are sanctuaries, sources of pleasure, power, and possibility for ourselves. A world where we remember that the Black body was created to be loved.

For too long, Black women have been told to make ourselves small, to swallow our screams, and to carry the burdens of a nation. But UNRULY summons another way. It is a celebration of our vastness, power, and unquenchable aliveness. It is a love letter to the parts of ourselves we have been taught to hide, the parts that refuse to be contained.

UNRULY is an offering, an altar, an uprising. It is a testament to the brilliance and resilience of Black women who have alchemized their suffering into art, and their trauma into testimony. It is a call to honor the wisdom of our bodies, and to listen to the stories our flesh holds. UNRULY bears witness to the unending grace and ferocity of our survival.

As you read these poems, I invite you to bring your own body to the page, to feel the heat and weight of each word in your own skin and bones. To reverently let yourself be broken open, undone, and remade. Through witness, I invite you to also embody the individual and collective work of healing and transformation that our world needs.

May these poems be a balm, even as they are a reckoning. May they remind us of the power that lies in our telling and the worlds that await us when we dare to speak our truths. May they call us home to ourselves, each other, and to the radical possibilities of our becoming.

Here, we bleed. Here, we birth ourselves. Here, we (re)claim.

The Akoma Ntoso, or "linked hearts," symbolizes understanding and agreement. It represents the connection between people and our shared experiences, reminding us that we are bound together in both struggle and healing.

I bleed
as my grandmothers bled.

THE BODY. IN PAIN.

Mt. Miegs, Alabama.

1845.

17-year-old Anarcha,
an enslaved African woman,
labored for three days. Birthing
left her bruised in the places
where only her God could see.
She now is a jagged opening
of the wall between her vagina
and bladder, being open
where others are permitted borders.
Her body, not her own, was torn and
transferred to the overseer for the wounded,
given over to another, again to labor
in the medical fields where doctors
had no training,

~~James. Marion. Sims.~~
Operated on Anarcha
to repair where she opened.
Operated on Anarcha for
four years. Operated on Anarcha
over thirty times. Operated
on Anarcha with no anesthesia.
Believed Black people did not feel
pain like White people. Did not
need anesthesia during surgeries
because ~~saviors~~ do not give more than
he can bear. In his autobiography,
he wrote, *There was never a time
that I could not, at any day, have had
a subject for operation.*

Anarcha could not write
her story. History will not recognize we have
presence when invisibility is the weapon
of choice. We have been subject to silences.

18-year-old Lucy almost met the final silence
after her first surgery, an hour of her opening,
blaspheming, screaming, crying out. Open
while a dozen presiding men, doctors, watched.
Could not stomach how *Lucy's agony was extreme.*
They had eyes to see too much, and never
returned because distance is a privilege.

The only other enslaved woman named
on record was Betsey. Betsey also suffered
from fistulas. Betsey also suffered from medical
experimentation. Betsey also suffered. Betsey
suffered. Betsey. Betsey. Bet sey. B e t s e y.
The many other enslaved women and children; young
women and children; women, children, and teenagers
are not
named, Betsey. The other girls and women are not
remembered, Betsey. He had a statue in Central Park,
Betsey. He has now moved to Brooklyn to stand erect
on his marked grave. Is still standing. Named. Betsey
is now of Alabaman soil. Mothered earth. We too
remain uncovered Betsey. Of his experiments, he said
this was the most *memorable time* of his life. Even in
death his view matters. You were not remembered.
Always birthing. Betsey, he is called the father
of gynecology, got his training by slicing our
wombs again and again and

again and again

and   again.

We were never meant to be a place of study
for others, our bodies. They have never asked for our
permission, even in the beginning Betsey, even if
we wanted to remain virgins. Our bodies will not
save you. Our bodies. Our bodies. He finally *perfected*
his technique, successfully *repaired* Anarcha's
fistula. Anarcha endured the infections,
surviving four years of being open.

New York, New York.

2017.

No one called my name
as I sat in a waiting room
from 9 a.m. – 2 p.m.
Sat in solitary confinement
with only My pain. It can
never be told well, it stole
my tongue. I lost my whole
mouth centuries before as I became
disfigured, distorted by our
agony and the doctor gave us
nothing. Black people do not feel
pain like white people.
I was feeling all of it.

The receptionist, a Black woman,
she saw me, asked if I got a prescription.
No one gave me anything. *Sit down baby*,
she said, and came back with relief,
600 mg of Ibuprofen, every six hours to take
the edge off. *She saw me* when my pain

gave me the power to disappear with what
can never be told well. It is a thief.

I searched for the other women suffering
in silence with their wandering wombs
and agony dismissed in cycles. I found
the stories they told. *Help! I am scared.*
What is happening to my body?

I saw three different ob-gyns
who just didn't understand
didn't want to understand.

Nobody was sympathetic
not even other women, friends,
thought I was exaggerating.

It feels like I have a pelvis
full of razor blades.

I internalized shame
and the taboo of speaking
up, which meant 20 years
of suffering with no diagnosis.

Found their stories buried
on a forum page for the care of
pet guinea pigs. Some of them wanted
death, wanted the edge off.

Guinea pigs can make the perfect companion because they do not take up much room and they are quiet. In the new owner's guide, we are reminded that in their silence, guinea pigs cannot always tell, in your language, what is wrong, so for those who give care it is useful to know what is healthy and what is not. Useful to know that the way we know to listen, or the way we expect them to tell, may not be a match. The telling of pain, in particular, can be a challenge because guinea pigs can hide pain really well. Can hide illness really well. Will conceal their wounds in ways we do not understand. They are prey animals. Any show of weakness means they may be chosen by a predator and eaten. They know to survive. And any day they have survived is a day to be celebrated.

Baltimore, Maryland.

2013.

The courts are trying to determine how much their pain is worth. They are having nightmares, are afraid to return to any doctor's office, have not been seen since they found out. Cannot see themselves. She is 67 and has not been to the gynecologist once since. These are crucial times, they say, but she can't be touched. She is young and naïve and ignored her intuition when he sent her chaperone out the room. She is haunted by the time he may not have used gloves. She only visited a new doctor to remove her gallbladder because she was forced to go to the emergency room. She will not send her children to be seen because no one in her family will be vulnerable that way again. They have taken their bodies out of the medical care system. She has stopped getting her annual blood tests for her thyroid problem. The sight of a white lab coat and a pen in the pocket brings anxiety. She has made several appointments but is now always a no-show. She will show no part of her skin, no one can look upon her but God. She scans every examination room for hidden cameras before she will disrobe. She has been vomiting. She can't bring herself to go back, lying there, exposed. She is healing herself by cutting herself deeper than the transgression. ~~Levy~~ recommended her hysterectomy, and she wants that part of herself back now. Cannot be made whole. More has been taken than body parts. She cries about her powerlessness to move time and space. She wants it to all go away. It started when he was hired in 1988 into a legacy of where things are taken without consent—Johns Hopkins—took HeLa cells because the grain of Black women's bodies resemble the distressed finish of auction blocks. This sin is antique. Our bodies are always being trespassed. Police have seized an extraordinary amount of evidence. They do not know how many women have been filmed, genitalia unknowingly put on display, legs in stirrups, asked to strip bare for their exam. ~~Levy~~ has seen through all of them. There are over 8,344 women. They are mostly poor and Black. They have been immortalized. Again.

The courts have settled on the figure of $190 million for the women in this East Baltimore clinic opened in 1979 to serve low-income residents. ~~Levy~~ was a popular Ob/Gyn, something about his warm nature put many women at ease, reminded them of Dr. Huxtable from the ~~Cosby~~ Show, everyone loved the idea of him, sent their daughters to him, sheep for the slaughter, referred him to friends and co-workers and sisters and cousins and communities of women for whom statistics on sexual violence suggest many have already experienced some type of abuse, and Johns Hopkins is terribly sorry this has happened. He has gone rogue. At least we will not build monuments to him. All patients of ~~Dr. Nikita Levy~~ will instead receive damages for their pain because they can get no justice, no closure, and no answers from his suicide note to his wife asking her to *please please please continue to love* him. He chose death because he did not want to see her suffer. Even in death his view mattered more. He has seen so much already. And there are women that did not want to be seen in those ways. This is one of the highest single sex perpetrator settlements in the history of the United States. This is one of the largest payouts of its kind.

The 8,344 plaintiffs will be placed in categories. Women in category one will get $1,750 because they have no negative experiences in their telling. They were the quietest. Category two will get $11,629. Category three will get $20,001. Category four will get $26,048 because they have told a history of severe abuse. Disclaimer: you will not be made whole. Disclaimer: victims will be categorized based on emotional distress, impact on life, and individual vulnerability. Disclaimer: we will not attempt to match you to the thousands of videos and images of genitalia because the fungibility of your bodies was not sanctioned, this time. Disclaimer: your category is determined by an interview and how well you tell your pain. Disclaimer: accepting your award means you cannot claim damages outside of this class action lawsuit. Disclaimer: accepting your award could impact your social security, Medicaid, or section 8 vouchers. Disclaimer: the settlement will be paid through its insurance policy and will not in any way compromise the ability of the health system to serve its patients, staff, and community. Disclaimer: you may never feel safe again. Disclaimer: your anger has no place here. Disclaimer:

The legal firms will get $32 million. This was a reduction from the $65 million they requested. Disclaimer: Your various legal teams were enormously appreciative to have been appointed to represent the thousands of victims. Disclaimer: dignity may continue to deny you.

Schochor, Federico and Staton Law Firm: *What Not to Say to* ~~*Dr. Levy*~~*'s and Johns Hopkins Hospital's Victims*

1. Don't tell them jokes.
2. Don't tell them, "It's just a picture."
3. Don't tell them how they could have avoided it.
4. Don't make fun of them.
5. Don't tell them it would never happen and why.
6. Don't avoid them.
7. Don't treat them like they have the plague.
8. Don't disbelieve them.
9. Don't tell them not to talk about it.
10. Don't tell them to put what happened out of their minds.
11. Don't pressure them into situations.
12. Don't tell them they are weak because it impacts their life.
13. Don't ask them what they are supposed to do to get past what happened.
14. Don't ask them if they could have done something different during the exams or picked a different doctor.
15. Don't tell them that it's not rape because it was just a picture.
16. Don't get mad if you give them a hug and they pull away.
17. Don't get mad if you're together and the victim has a flashback.
18. Don't be afraid to talk to them if they're upset.

19. Don't be afraid of them.
20. Don't tell them they should take it as a compliment.

Washington Post: *A gynecologist secretly photographed patients. What's their pain worth?*

2017 Comments:

1. **observator1000:** "If they had no idea then why was it so traumatic when they found out? In the world we live in today, nudity is nothing."

2. **LiberalFreedomFighter:** "Murders earn victim's families far less money for a much more serious crime."

3. **ustekinumab:** "This whole case is hysteria and greedy lawyers. The women should have gotten $500 and nothing more. Too bad if they are over-emotional wrecks."

4. **dkb50:** "This is a pretty lucrative settlement for each of them. It's a great payout for an injury that involves no physical suffering. I suspect they'll get over it pretty quick when the money is in their hands."

5. **alert4jsw:** "And if nudity—even if undesired—can be the source of this much 'trauma,' maybe we need to work on our society's inability to relate to our natural state."

6. **ustekinumab:** "This is about extorting Johns Hopkins and screwing the public. These women knew that the doctor was going to examine their

vaginas. You know how BLACKS work the system, don't ya?"

7. **Raemike:** "I'm sorry they are suffering so much, but there are far worse situations and many victims have real traumas that will never see a nickel of retribution."

8. **Icky Schwartz:** "Women have to learn that they, and their sisters are all constructed the same way. Seen one, you've seen them all. Get over it."

9. **judy_p01:** "This would not destroy my dignity and sense of safety."

10. **LaborLawyer:** "The psychological trauma these women suffered is the result of Victorian societal standards that put women on pedestals and assumes women to be fragile flowers."

11. **flowman164:** "I'm guessing that being secretly photographed by a perverted gynecologist is probably not the worst thing that's happened to these poor black women. But it's the thing they're getting paid for."

12. **LiberalFreedomFighter:** "$190 million for embarrassment?
Wow.
That's absurd."

13. **Mettleandgrit:** "These women are inventing psychological problems just to cash in."

14. **OObuck:** "Are we really so fragile, or are we just into victimhood? Time to get on with your life."

15. **PIA9:** "I wonder how many women's lives were saved by this doctor?"

16. **Raemike:** "This will impact an incredible organization and many people for a nearly victimless crime."

17. **Dan MD:** "Make Gynecology Expensive Again"

18. **Smithereens:**
"That sh*t is illegal.
It's a violation.
Patient privacy
is sacrosanct—
except
apparently
when those
whose privacy
was violated
are Black
women, and
those judging
them are
not."

I promised no doctor
would touch me again, yet she,
this body, keeps making me
into a liar.

New York, New York.

2018.

The hospital has never been a welcoming place, but I fear I am making it a home. My lexicon is now expert with the word chronic, or infinity, the alpha and the omega, or the many ways there is no end. No one notices my tears here. *Take a seat.* This home reeks of a violence as sterilized as the homes where I grew up. To be home again is to be overcome. *Roll up your sleeve.* My numbers are telling the stories of those who have survived the Middle Passage with its diet of salt and suffering and how we are now vulnerable to high blood pressure. It is an unnatural selection. I got good genes. *Look straight ahead.* I tell the nurse that those numbers are because I am here, again, trying to forget my mothers. *Open your mouth.* Your names are on my tongue Anarcha, Lucy, Betsey. They bound my wrist with my name and the date my flesh came into this world. I dress in the gown that leaves my back exposed. *Take a deep breath.* My body is remembering, for all of us, how I would wet the bed even as a teenager, and the doctors could never understand why my bladder would empty herself. At least my piss could run. *Have you been out of the country lately?* Science does not know how to measure the ways I have tried to survive. I have only come home because my other home has been bleeding. *What brought you here today?* This body is becoming inhospitable. I give myself over because I am desperate for rest from these rough waters. *Open your mouth.* The ancestors are preparing a place for me. The laying on of hands. I welcome being called to the home that was promised, where I am no longer the body. *Take a deep breath.* Let not your heart be troubled.

I bleed
where there are no openings.

DIAGNOSIS

luckily, you stayed
fought for your life
as if you could
do anything else
morphine induced
muffled screams
demand nothing less
of this world
luckily, we listened
heard
interrupted

.

unnecessary
unwarranted
unsuitable
unconvincing
uninteresting
unpredictable
unrecognizable
unacknowledged
unidentifiable
unforeseen
unintentional
unseen
undeniable
uncovered
unremarkable

could be cancer

.

WEARING WHITE

Once, when I was becoming
a woman, the doctor asked
about you.
She had a clipboard, pen,
the privilege of distance.
Your last bleed?
Your symptoms?
Want a pill to go with that?
Then it was time
to put you under
a microscopic glare.

Once, when I was becoming
a goddess, the doctor examined
the source of life in me.
She had a speculum,
and my future
weighing on her shoulders.
Anyone ever tell you?
She called you a textbook uterus
and I smiled,
an unearned achievement.

Once, I was immortal.

AFTER BREONNA

every new moon
I squat and spread
my legs above my mother
and empty my self into her

already knows our taste
we kin, salt, rusted
we who toil, we earth
she holds us in her belly

this, corporeal offering, warm,
like how we once gave her back
our almost daughters, to hold,
and I wonder when I will stop

being afraid of blood memory

ODE TO MY BELLY

the first time you were swollen
before my first bleed at 13
when my pants no longer fit
I cried about my own evolution
and thought I was pregnant
with the third coming of Jesus

that my now swollen belly
must be involuntarily carrying
the virgin seed of a savior
for this world conceived
immaculately and I fretted
how I would tell people
I was that important
to have been chosen

little Black belly of mine
full of grace
and then the blood
left wine-colored stains
in my floral print panties
because I was unprepared
for my body to be so ordinary
for this world to be so ordinary

and I have had to learn you
little Black belly of mine
and your cycles over and over again
and dress you according to your whims
and I have had to learn how to love
every woman I am becoming

LEVITICUS

An atonement
for her
uncleanness.
A woman
an issue
her issue
her flesh
her blood.
A woman
shall be unclean
and everything
every   thing
any thing
whosoever touch
be unclean
          separation
                  separation
                          separation
          separation
                                    be   unclean.
                          If a woman
                          has an issue of
              blood   runs beyond
                          all the days of
                          her uncleanness,
                              her issue
                          shall be unto her
                              all the days.
                          Her issue
                          shall be unto her
                          an atonement.

DIAGNOSIS

Who told you
you had cancer?
No, this is suffering
by another name.

Endometriosis.
Stage IV.
Chocolate Cyst.
8 x 10 cm.

There is no cure
for this. No metaphor
for this. No other way
to say this.

IT GROWS WHEREVER IT WANTS

Once, I was immortal.
Then you grew me
pink flowers,
death blossoms.

You signal the season's end
with a full harvest
of your engorged fruit.

Flesh of my flesh,
bone of my bone,
what do I know of cycles
when you will not wilt?

CHOCOLATE CYST

seeking someone special to spend my life with. Are you kissed by the sun and are of the darker skin hue? Are you invisible even when your cells are viewed under a microscope? Can you carry me annually without anyone noticing? Can you carry yourself and be told you do it so well that you are an inspiration? Are you used to carrying too much history in your bones? Do they call you strong, or loud, or angry, or intimidating as a way to silence you? Do they say you have no pain? Do they say you have no right to express your pain? If so, then I may be your match! I am the kind of presence that will not leave your (in)side. You say you want someone to grow with you, but what's even better is I will grow throughout you. I will leave no part of you untouched by my reach. Every inch of you will know I am with you. We will spend our days in bed, leaving this world to wonder what fire has consumed you so. I am a match. I will light up every part of you and your world so that we can spend more time together alone. We will spend our nights entangled, tossing and turning. And when the day breaks, and breaks, and breaks, and breaks, and breaks you, I will not leave you.

YOUR WITNESS HAS NO EYES

I had a chance to greet death, sit down and commune
with her, was not as gentle as I thought she'd be,

was invasive—
At the market today, there was an amazing sale, like the

like the memory you convinced yourself you had
forgotten, or the secret never meant

for your ears, yet it was yours even when you tried
to give it away. She knew my secrets, called me

by my name, a slow drawl—
Can you believe winter is coming so soon, in slow drawls?

the slow drawl of an encroaching fog, becoming
invisible to everyone but myself. Pressed

my wet palm against my breast to feel life still
cycling through me, and finding little comfort in

my solitary hand—
The best part was when he saved her and took her by the hand.

I remember the iridescence,
and being frightened by my solitary view.

If this world has demanded
your silence
your body
your participation
in your flesh being torn away
sold to market among bruised plums
too sweet to eat quickly,
then your rebellion will be
in every breath
every tear drop
every laugh that has escaped
from the lips of our children.

—ANARCHA

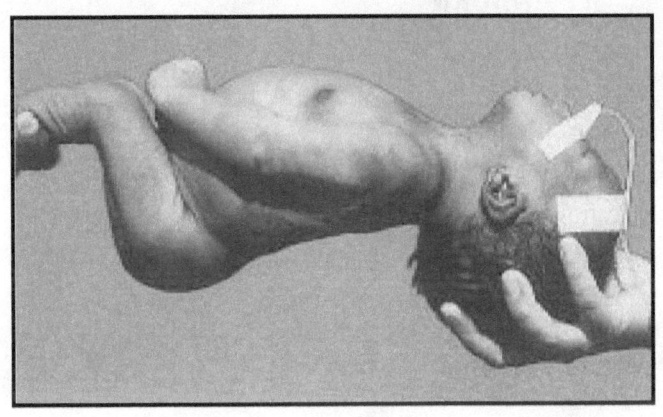

I bleed.
 I bleed.
I bleed.
 I bleed.
I bleed.
I bleed.
 I bleed.
  I bleed.
 I bleed.
I bleed
 I blee
  I ble
 I bl
  I b
  I
  i
  .

ODE TO MY UNBORN

I saw you
in my dreams
counted your
whispered fingers,
one for every year
we wanted to
expect you,
the discerning visitor
who would not
come. The doctor
said I was
a mess in there.
Emptiness

was never
welcome here.
Every month
a runway;
red
carpet
of clots
and solitude.
Here in this place
I have carved out
for you, among
my scars I have
prepared a place
for you. The doctors
say it will take
a Herculean effort
to bring you
into this world,
as if our bodies are
mythology.

THE MOTHERS ARE ON MY TONGUE

For Mary Turner and her unborn child,
lynched in Lowndes County, Georgia, 1918

It is said that they *clamored* to be seen by the butcher.
When promises are spoken that are as sweet as

mist in a world of fire and brimstone then fungible
bodies move without consent in the direction of he

who has the most to gain from their possession. It is
said those were the times, that the end justifies

the means because grace is always given to them
who are permitted their humanity. They never

wanted to be the mothers of gynecology, never
coveted the brutality, or how this world will flourish

from their pain, or for their names to be buried
in our amnesia. They only wanted to mother

themselves into being, without lashes and plantations,
without vaginal tears and breeding. There was never

a time to be vulnerable. The mothers want to be
known as the mothers of soft things and beauty.

ODE TO IDA MAE

Your hair has a way it waves to the wind,
a performance that ends in my company as you peel
back your wig to expose who is underneath,

exhaling as though you have been holding your breath
all day. Your bones creak as you lower yourself to sit.
Chile, come over here and scratch my scalp.

Cradling your head back I undo the thick braids on the top
of your disheveled white crown, part your hair to reveal

the dryness of your scalp, and you tell me of an itch
you cannot reach with your own hands. You breathe
a sigh of relief even as the comb breaks through skin.
Stay right there chile! You're the one place I am safe with no name.
You bleed as red as the blood from the keloids on your back.

I do not know if I can ever get to the depth of that ache.
Your face twists, we accept defeat, this is enough digging
for one day. I rub grease into your thirsty roots,
plait your hair tightly so it can hold
until we commune again at the kitchen table.

GENESIS

     The deep   waters
separated   separated   separated
     And it was so.

The   seed-bearing
    sacred
created   and   blessed
          there
    and there

in our image
    created   created   every seed
           every   seed
everything that has   breath   life

    And   And   And   And
    it   it   it   it
    was   was   was   was
so.   so.   so.   so.

ODE TO MY WRISTS

These wrists
cannot stand the burden
of bangles that feel
so much like chains.
14 karats of bondage
on a body remembering
I could only press into
you with the dull edges
of plastic cutlery.
This world does not
welcome your kind
though you are going
nowhere.

These wrists
washed in the blood
of needles that have pierced
your skin again and again
to remind you of the fire
that forms, the rise,
the ashes. You always
transform the scars into
testimony. She who came
into being by herself
in a world that honors
only one resurrection.

DEAR GYNECOLOGIST,

There were so many times I prepared for death. Like when my waters broke with a force that pushed past the boughs of my staples. First, I leaked then ran to the bathroom to take a piss and found instead I was breaking open. I stood there, half-naked, panties around my ankles. I was a flood of mysterious waters and tears. Drowning is never convenient. And the woman I call my grandmother, born in Alabama, tried to save me from my own tides. I ebb and flow and flow and flow and flow. She called me by my childhood name. *Chile, why don't you move?* I was immobilized. *Chile, move.* I was being emptied out. *Chile, what should I do?* And I stood there, crying in this torrential body of mine. Broken. Open. And I wondered why you never told me how to prepare for the hurricanes. She put newspapers on the floor between my legs. Legs spread eagle. I had no more modesty in me as I soiled her floors with my insides. I could not be contained by the bikini cut incision with the staples that understood *I release all things that no longer serve me.* All I could do was stare down between my legs. I was everywhere, and nowhere. And I noticed the neighborhood C-Town Supermarket is having a sale on cantaloupes. I have had my own orchard cut out of me. I have had enough with fruits.

THE METAMORPHOSIS   (OR PHRONESIS)

Lying in bed I grow uncomfortable at how bone presses against bone. The pain of kneecaps grinding against one another in child's pose made sleep impossible the night before. I have not stepped on a scale lately, have no energy to take more than a few steps a day, but somehow, I know I must have spent weeks wasting away. The only time it felt good to laugh was when I put on a once tight skirt only to watch it slowly slouch down to my ankles while finding no frame to hold onto. I am no more, and yet I marvel at how the body has become so determined to live, even when the soul starts to dream of that next place. I am not sure who will greet me on the other side—maybe the mothers—but I know I no longer feel welcome in this pain body.

My husband gently lifts me out of bed, taking breaks to let me adjust the pelvic weight of the watermelon-size tumor so I could walk to the bathroom. Today is the day I am scheduled to have surgery and in honor of the occasion I thought it best to shower. Everything hurts. Even the warm streams of water on my skin feel like punishment, and when the torture of touch is over, I declare myself ready.

There is nothing that could have prepared me for traversing the New York City streets. The city is too bustling with life to welcome someone like me, someone who walks with death. Every pothole is an atom bomb inside of me. Every red light, a personal attack. Every taxi driver in a rush towards life, a slap in the face. I close my eyes and hum Old Negro Spirituals hoping the ancestors hear in the silences that I too am ready to come home. *I wanna be ready. / I wanna be ready. / I wanna be ready.*

When I arrive at the hospital, I notice how the pace of life continues to speed past. Doctors speak at my body. My hand signs papers, as though she has authority to give away organs if they determine the tumor is cancerous. I am asked every question except how I am doing. I am scared. I am no more.

My husband says when I woke from my drugged sleep I hummed before I could speak. A low hum connecting me to a time before language. Speaking in tongues. And when I spoke, to the living, my first words were that I'd been split in half. And when I saw the metal holding my lower half intact with my upper half, I cried out that I was a monster.

I bleed
to make a way out of no way.

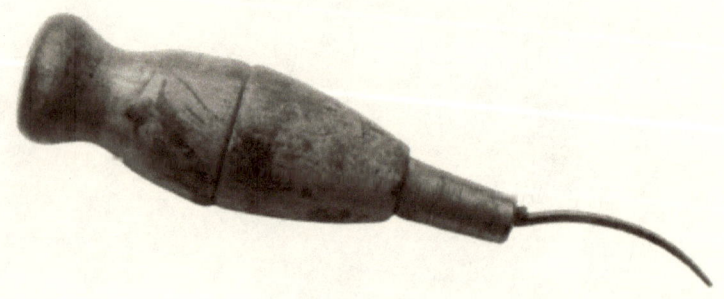

THE SHOEMAKER'S AWL

The good doctor, father butcher, wanted to *cure* the Black babies of their Blackness. Diagnosed them with a moral weakness that advancement in medicine will come to call *neonatal tetanus*. He, the patron saint of slaughter and sacrifice, was troubled by the laziness of infancy prevailing among the Black children who thought Alabama air was free. The mothers, with legs spread eagle, wailed, their babies covered in *vernix caseosa* and the plantation's poverty. Beautiful Black babies coming into this world, through blood and the breaking of water too close to hell and horse shit. Did he even swab the soiled crowns of their heads with his saliva as reverence? The children cry at the touch of foreign hands, and he holds her young, gently at first, by the skull. Finds the place not yet hardened, still open to this world. Puts the shoemaker's awl at the crown, still malleable, still warm. Presses down to loosen the bones. Down. Down. Down. Down. Down. Down to pry apart the skull, soft as leather, into a *proper* alignment. And it was so.

My children
my children
my children
tear through me
eager to become
bone, flesh.
Eager to exhale me.
I give my breast
to a world that robs
the earth of its roots.
Try to soothe myself
with my own milk
latch on to my own life
rock my self to sleep at night.

— *BETSEY*

DEAR MOTHER,

When I asked my older brother why he did not help, he said it was because they *liked* me. Stood there and let those two neighborhood boys touch me like that. The soon to be men were shocked how possessed I was by mania as I wrestled myself free while calling for my *Mommy*. Showed you my torn clothes, my still wet face, my fright in broad daylight. And I didn't even have breasts then. In bare feet you bolted outside, running on sidewalks of broken glass and crack vials. Other daughters collected Barbie dolls, or Cabbage Patch Kids, but I curated paraphernalia because the colors were so pretty. I remember when you found my exquisite crack vial display in my room, you threw everything out the window without a word. Made me wash my hands to bring back innocence. For days I stared at the fractured rainbow on the ground beneath my windowsill. It had taken me weeks to gather that treasure. You ran like a gazelle, swinging your slotted spoon with red sauce over our heads. Grabbed one of the boys by his collar. Twisted it until your fist was at his neck. I was moved by how beautifully and viciously you love. You with your vile tongue and your unwillingness to let that boy go. In your anger I learned I was a holy place. And for supper, we two little Black girls say our grace, break bread together, and wipe away the red sauce from our silent, hungry faces.

THE AFTERBIRTH

I wanted to love you
up close, bare
souled.
You gave me your hand
to hold,
said *put it to your bosom*
and I shuddered,
hesitated
to receive the comfort
of your touch.
The lion is a beautiful animal
when seen at a distance
and I will not bleed out.

THE BODY IN PAIN

My Black momma
with her black belt
whooping my Black ass
to give me something
to cry about.   As if
I haven't already
been emptied
of my tears.   As if
my essence
could ever be seen
and not heard.   As if
beating me like
a runaway slave
teaches me love.   As if
the good Lord would give
strength to your hands
already too heavy.   As if
the ritual of choosing
my own switch
will soothe the pain.   As if
knocking the taste
out of my mouth
will soothe your pain.   As if
rebuking the sound
of my cries
will soothe your pain.   As if
fixing my face to not
resemble my father's
will soothe your pain.   As if
threatening to take me
out of this world
will soothe your pain.   As if
my Blackness
could ever be

knocked off.   As if
                      as if
                      as if

I live in a world
that loves me
too much.

DEAR MOTHER,

There was a time when I practiced what to call you. *Mom* no longer fit in my mouth without twisting the corners into the shape of rebellion. A near asphyxiation by silence. I would inhale deeply as I searched for my lost breath. Then I tried to carefully trace *Mom/my* with my tongue and found it retreated to the back of my throat. Could it be I had become so expert at being seen and not heard that I would sometimes throw away my own mouth? My teenage crush also left me without a mouth. He would stare with his hazel eyes waiting for me to answer the questions I never heard because I was also left without ears. I was a crime scene. There were pieces of me. What remained was disconnected from my senses. *Chile act like she ain't got no good sense.* I stared back with eyes that did not see and shrugged a shoulder to say, *I don't know,* to questions I did not hear. I was skilled at disappearing. It was safer that way. A boy referred to me once as *the retarded girl who does not speak.* He was not trying to be mean; he was only trying to understand how it was I became endangered and then extinct so quickly. As if by choice.

As if I was born to be a shadow, so no one really knew what to do with a girl. A girl becoming a woman. A human being. Being. To be, without permission, is sometimes considered a threat. To save myself I had to disappear you. I started with your name.

ODE TO MY THIGHS

The boys, seeing how skinny I was, would swim over to me playing
their games, dunking all the girls along the way to show how
    power operates.
You wrap around them until their skin burns, and as their nostrils
fill with chlorinated water they marvel at your impenetrable build.

Said I was no fun. As if submission is a game to enjoy.
You come from a people who were taken. Survival is in your
    DNA, but they
are still too young to understand this kind of strength, how you
    are to be
worshipped like storms with your thunder thighs that stir
    everything asleep

to wake. Yet, they have not learned to behold the beauty of your
    unruliness.
They laugh as your muscles pump in the double-dutch ropes, call
you horse legs because they're afraid of you discovering yourself.
    Every sinew
wanted to know freedom because you were never made to be
    conquered.

Yet, they are determined to have dominion, so tag, you're it. But
    not even
the winds dare stand in your way as you run past every one of
    them with no
broken sweat. This is the consecration. You have had enough with
    running
away. You make the galaxies quake and no longer stay where you
    are not loved.

DEAR MOTHER,

After he raped me.
After he finished raping me.
After the raping.
After the rape occurred.
After we finished having sex.
After he had sex with me.
After he had sex.
After the sex.
After it happened. After it stopped. After he stopped.
After he fucked. After the fucking. After being fucked.
Over.
After he climbed off and gave me a kiss.
Also unwanted.
After trying to forget while it was still happening. I came
close to forgetting. After being thanked for a good time.
After being thankful he used a condom, used protection while
using me. After opening
my eyes. After seeing my self in the ceiling mirror sprawled out on a
heart-shaped bed wondering if this is what romance was supposed
to feel like. I must have missed that chapter in the puberty book—
What's Happening to My Body?— you mysteriously left on my bed
when my shape was changing. After I saw my heart sprawled out,
budding blossoms in a training bra that could no longer hold me.
After acting like I liked it because I was afraid his ego was too
brittle. *What's happening to my body?* After I lost
my humanity.
After he left the room, I think I covered my self. I think I finally
exhaled.
After his friend came into the room next. After his friend stood in
the corner and looked ashamed
to see me breaking. After being seen. Broken.
After the four of us got into the cab to return home, he was still
hungry. This was our double date. Also unwanted. After my *girl
friend* upset him with her no, would not let him touch her in the

motel with the heart-shaped beds, nor in the backseat of the cab; she had already been fucked once that night by the one who looked at me with shame in the crust of his eyes. All passages change you. After being kicked out of the cab it was just the two of us girls in the middle of nowhere. After asking my *friend*. After asking a *friend*. After asking this girl. After asking her why she invited me out earlier that night. After asking if she knew we were never going to the movies that night. After asking if she knew I always stayed away from him. After she apologized. Mother, you said you would never apologize to me. I remember your resolve. After she asked that we never speak of this night again, I gave away my tongue. I was the keeper of your secrets too. After decades of silence. After gathering more wounds along the way. *What is happening to my body?* I told you. That night that blurred into my becoming a woman. After you told me the same thing happened to you. There was no crack in your voice though and the sun was bright, and I felt blinded. I realized my sorrow had no place here. After I heard how dry your face was over the phone, I came to love the torrents inside of me.

ESTROGEN DOMINANCE

Doctors in Italy have found a link between beauty and suffering.
Have said too much estrogen leads to endometriosis.
Have said too much estrogen leads to beauty.
Have said that to be full of beauty is to be full of oneself,
a proliferating self,
a fatal attraction.

DEAR MOTHER,

That summer I was mystified how, after coming out of the Harlem pool, the other little Black girls still had straight hair. My wet hair, instead, took the long journey from touching my shoulders to passing the burnt skin of my ears—since I never learned to sit still—only to return home to the crowded kitchen at the nape of my neck. I wanted so much to also stand in the sprinklers without descending into otherness; to smell like their freedom rather than Sulfur-8. How I lamented having hair so thick it kept breaking all your good combs. When you grew tired of the strength of my hair, you gave me a Jheri Curl and a pleather jacket like MJ. And I was cute too, until the school nurse saw the chemical burns on the back of my neck where my kitchen should have been and sent me home early. In the gym, a classmate, ashamed of their ashy legs after we changed into shorts, asked if they could rub my head to get some of the curl activator to use as lotion. All those chemicals and I didn't even go to the pool anymore, even after graduating to hair relaxers that would burn my scalp, leaving scabs all over my crown after touch-ups every eight to ten weeks. *Studies have shown that hair relaxers can cause fibroids and an early onset of puberty in girls.*

ODE TO MY LIPS

In the dead of winter, I spoke a word that did not want to be
heard and my lip was busted open because my mouth needed

to be closed and the red of my blood melted through all
that was pure. And then I learned how to suck in my lips,

and I would look like a Whyte girl who was protected
by this world. My long hair was made of a 100% cotton

towel I would flip while standing in front of the mirror
to hide the curl of my kink. I was starting to accept my own

invisibility when I found red lipstick, but the boys laughed,
said I looked like a clown because my lips were too full

of themselves. My first kiss was the back of a hand.
And my lips would always pout because they were

swollen from too much truth. Yet still I will never
understand silence.

DEAR DAUGHTER,

Who gave you the right to escape from this prison? Who told you you could be happy? That it was within your reach? Are you a child of mine? If so, then we cannot recognize your face. It is too beautiful, too strong, too confident. The face we created was marred with the tears that watered plantations from Mt. Miegs, Alabama, to the sugarcane fields of Falmouth, Jamaica. You were always crying in ways that felt biblical even though we salvaged you from the precious metals of the bridle / muzzle / mask / bit that covered our mouths, tamed our tongues, and cut into our skin to suffocate hunger. Are you a child of mine? Did your mouth not learn to be caged? Are your cries prophecy or omen? We cannot recognize your face. Still, why do your eyes glimmer with a hope after our blood fertilized these lands? Take, eat, these are our bodies.

And the women are to pluck out both eyes in the name of honor. And the women and the women and the women are to know their place after Eden's fall. Child, this is not the right time for freedoms. You are no child of mine. You do not wear our mark of pain and we cannot recognize that smile.

I
bleed
because
our bodies
have stories
to tell

.

SHE WHO HAD BEEN SCATTERED THROUGH TIME

If I die   bury me
with my clitoris
re-attached
gather up
my pieces
make them
whole
reclaim the lost
and found
I am
the peasant boy
the queen
from pharaoh
to slave
birth
to grave
I am the beauty
and the agony
the rapture
the shame
the deceived
and the blamed
I am the salvation
springtime with roses
and earthquakes
too deep for a richter scale
I am freedom
and keloids
from whipped
and beaten souls
nothing masking my pain
this is all of me
beautiful,   scarred

A LIVING SACRIFICE

take   this is my body breaking for you
leaving no blood on your white coats I bow
prostrate with pain and learning to perish

among the broken I come to you an
offering of bitter cups I cannot
take this is my body breaking for you

to make room for the benign ruins of life
growing without having been sowed bodies
prostrate in pain and learning to perish

within my womb I lay here spread eagle
with your silences between my thighs you
take this is *my* body breaking for you

and your instrument's gaze too cold to see
what afflicts eternities of bodies
prostrate with pain still learning to perish

this do in suppression of me because
there is no more pleasure in remaining
take my   broken
                pain   perishing

PERHAPS YOU ARE ALREADY BROKEN

Perhaps the room is empty to make room, it must be courteous, after all, for when the doctor says I must open just a little bit wider. He maps me. Gets lost in me. *Perhaps it is in hiding?* Like ovaries can be afflicted with shyness or run from the light. *Perhaps it will show itself on your next exam? Perhaps there is nothing to worry about?* Perhaps I should not have laughed out loud, been amused by the thought of a timid ovary playing hide-and-go-seek. Perhaps there is something to learn from this. Perhaps you will survive this. Perhaps God is trying to tell you something. Perhaps suffering is all in the mind. Perhaps you will get stronger if this does not kill you. Perhaps this is a dream, and you will wake soon. Perhaps this is a nightmare. Perhaps you will not survive this. Perhaps this is a curse. Perhaps you can still have children. Perhaps you deserve this. Perhaps you are holding onto too much of your past. Perhaps this is because of your mother. Perhaps this is because you do not know your father. Perhaps this is what will finally break you, perhaps your splintered self has pierced this world, perhaps this world needs you to remember its fragility, perhaps this world does not want to remember, perhaps this world can no longer look in your direction, perhaps everyone has to look away when your pain stares without manners. Perhaps the earth spins on its axis and seasons reappear and a baby bird cries out for its life in the mouth of a serpent with pollen traveling on its skin, shed, and left behind in a wilderness of poppies meant for your veins, crying out for your life. Perhaps there is no god
like my god. Perhaps she has called your name too soon. Perhaps you heard her misspeak and answered another's call. Perhaps you missed your calling. Perhaps you do not listen, or do not speak, or are not heard, or do not know the language of grace. Perhaps this was not grace. Perhaps you will laugh at this   someday.

HOW TO SURVIVE RAPE

Tell yourself to moan in order to shield his fragility; otherwise, he will call this rejection too. Tell yourself you didn't enjoy it and will not choose him again, as if you chose him in the first place. Tell yourself you chose him. Tell yourself you will not be a statistic and then protect yourself by separating your mind from your body. Try. Tell yourself the disassociation you practiced as a child can help you here. Go for a walk in the storms— always without cover—so you will finally have permission to mourn. Tell yourself this is working and that those aren't tears on your face mixed with the rain. Bury the memory inside of your cells. Say *I'm sorry* for crying if something triggers you like watching a pigeon playing hard to get. Mating season has its brutalities. Tell yourself what he said was true, that you were playing hard to get. Tell yourself it isn't rape if you played hard to get for a long enough time. Tell yourself that attrition is courtship. Bury the memory inside of your cells. Program your body to get wet so the next time it won't hurt so much. Train the salivation of your wetness like Pavlov's dog. Fear will be your stimulus. Tell yourself that preparing in this way is what it means to be turned on. Bury the memory inside of your cells. Let your body transmute the traumas into fibroid tumors. A recent study finds that *80-90% of Black women have had fibroids*, so this is normal. Tell yourself this is metamorphosis. Who are you becoming? Tell yourself you are not your body. That your body was never yours to begin with anyway. Tell yourself that owning your body is the biggest threat to man. Tell yourself that owning your body is a sin. Tell yourself that your heart wasn't in it, and he missed out on the best part of you. *Let not your heart be troubled.* Tell yourself it was only your body and that you didn't get hurt. Bury the memory inside of your cells. Tell yourself that your cells are not always remembering.

FIBROIDS

each time
our skin continues to heal
our skin continues to heal
the medical studies have
discovered that fibroid tumors
have the same biological
traits as keloid scars
they are reparative
they are reactive
tissues
our skin
our skin
that our cells
continue to signal
because our bodies
have been taught
that unconditional love
means going back
to where you hurt
skin
our only treatment
is to watch and wait
skin
skin
we got
good genes
skin
skin
skin
connective
tissue
skin
skin
skin

~~skin~~
excessive
~~skin~~
~~skin~~
~~skin~~
~~skin~~
~~skin~~
unceasingly
~~until mountains arose~~
~~as our unruly surfaces~~

DEAR 5LB BAG OF BUCKWHEAT,

My husband told me what he did to you. You have to understand, he was alone when I was in the hospital. Was afraid in a way that was new. He needed something to blame. Needed someone to be wrong. Someone had to answer for what was happening to me, the pain. I think he asked the air *why* because he could not find a god, but when he looked up, he only saw you. He tried to find your face. He does not look away in a fight and you angered him more with your silence. He had to find your face. He was a man with blood in his eyes where tears could have been.

I should have known that anything called the smother crop could not be tamed, inside of me. I prepared you well, waiting for the rolling boil to soften your rigid seed. But in my belly, you felt more like conquest than consumption. You swelled inside of me. A rolling boil stirred up what was dormant, inside of me. I cried enough for all of us.

Before what happened
happened
there was a fluttering inside
of me. Seemed like my spirit
already knew him to be mine
seemed like intoxication
the feeling of owning
something
someone all for myself
except he gave himself
to me. Gave himself.
To me. We possessed
each other, as best we could.
Created together, as best
we could. Then it happened.
And my poor butterflies,
their remains poison
my insides.

— LUCY

DEAR WASBAND,

In college, while wearing spandex, a classmate asked what exercises I did to strengthen my calf muscles. With a confused look on my face I responded, *exercises?* Maybe we can call it an unnatural selection since I was born in the same Jamaican parish as Usain Bolt. I got good genes. My kind of fortitude was bred over the centuries on sugar plantations and survival. I knew myself to be resilient, and this is why I always came back to you. *'Til death do us part.* Something happened on that surgery table. Every man profiled on MadameNoire spoke about how much he loves the Black woman for her resilience. They witnessed their mommas never show how much they were breaking, so it was only while I slept the pain was permitted to escape from my lips. You had trouble sleeping because the sounds I made were unbearable. We have always been valued for how much we can carry, like it is a compliment, but even the Christ who carried the cross to his own crucifixion is admired for how he can love. I want to say, *I am tired*, and have this world believe me. I cried before as a little girl, showed my pain, and my mother responded, *What are you, a whyte girl?* I never understood why tear ducts were a privilege, but I did not cry when I was admitted to the ER again one year after surgery. Not a tear was shed when the doctor did not give me pain meds, again. I know how to endure; this is why I am loved. This is how I love.

For   months

I will   not bleed.

Let the cycles be

broken.

DEAR WASBAND,

It takes something to love the wound. You need a certain range, like how I can sing in soprano then drop low to hit a note so deep and dark that it's easy to forget about my fragility. Ever since the staples were removed, and I tried to hold my self together, I wondered what it would be like to love my self with the everything I have given to a man. With the everything I have given to a momma. With the everything I have given to an everything. These are selfish times, yet I only know how to give myself away. When the infection set in, the E.coli, and they had to open me back up, I cried out, *Why me? What's happening to my body?* A doctor held my hand, in silence, while another pressed against my Black belly to release the toxicity that now refuses to stay inside. You looked away. Who are you becoming? The doctors were concerned for you, asked you to sit. *Breathe, sir.* / The mothers are with me on the examination table, *I release all things that no longer serve me.* / *Take a deep breath, sir.* I need you to know I do not crave immortality. I will have no beautiful eulogy praising my longsuffering, will no longer be revered for the broadness of my back even if it is not good that man should be alone. When the visiting home nurse stuffed gauze into my belly every day, I had to practice surrender to a new god. *Let no man possess you again.* It takes something to love a wounded woman. For six weeks, they kept my body open until the infection drained. This is the consecration. I have had to learn every woman I have become.

HYMNAL

If God's eye is on
the New York City pigeon
singing on my fire escape
at 5 o'clock in the morning
after I am released
from the hospital,
then I know that He
watches over me,
or the pieces of me,
held together
by prayer
and staples.

DEAR FORMER EMPLOYER,

My ovaries told me to quit. Told me to not concern myself with how to pay the light bill or how to put food on the table. In fact, I was already dressed for our workday, about to walk out the front door when I fell to the floor. Prostrate. My ovaries told me I was going nowhere. Told me, *breathe.* Told me, *be still.* I was not alone, for they were still with me, as I lay on the floor. We spent days gathering our strength. We were a crime scene. And when I could stand again, they told me, *Walk right into her office and break her heart.* I would have wanted to stay, but a woman has got to listen to her ovaries, especially when they protest as loud as mine do, demand so much attention. This is the consecration.

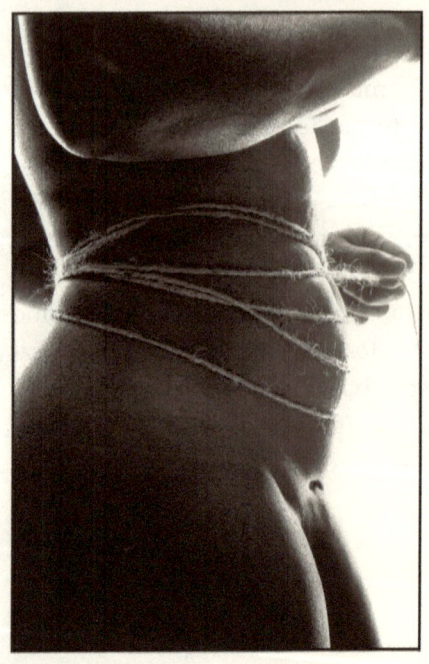

The sacred
has become
suffering.

I bleed.

WHERE WATER IS NOT BEGGED FOR

Each month,
in the season of
release, shards fall
from these brittle branches.
I did not choose this fire
sermon, do not stand for
a cause, and cannot find
peace in this body
as the flames consume.

You, wise one, chose
your match, doused your robes
in oil and the crackle of flesh
and bone became
your final meditation.
The flames engulfed
your ineffable silence
as your body, statuesque,
entered a peaceful trance.

Teach me.

FIBROIDS

Our bodies, in her infinite wisdom
could never pretend as though

all was well, even as we smile and
move mountains in that world

with ease, we got good genes.
Our bodies are the most honest

part of us, cannot pretend that
that world does not salivate

at our exploits and our birthings
and our babies and our tongues.

We were always worth more
because of what came through

us. Nothing that was gathered in that
world was given over to us, except

for the thorns. Flowers
that pollinate can yield

much harvest if you keep
the flower alive long enough.

Our bodies have had enough. Our
bodies in her infinite wisdom

have grown thorns, and keeps
growing them. Our bodies in her

infinite wisdom wants us to know

she grew the thorns on purpose.

Asè. Wants us to know she
heard our cries. Asè. Wants us

to know she protected us
the best way she could. Asè. Wants

us to know the language of flowers,
or fruits, or bodies, or soft things now.

Did she know pleasure? Did they hold each other? Did anyone miss her? Was her absence noticeable? Was her presence noticeable? Did she love another? Was she loved? Did she have desires? Did she call this punishment or healing? Was this pain greater than the lash? Did she know pleasure? Did they hold each other? Did anyone miss her? Was her absence noticeable? Was her presence noticeable? Did she love another? Was she loved? Did she have desires? Did she call this punishment or healing? Was this pain greater than the lash? Did she know pleasure? Did they hold each other? Did anyone miss her? Was her absence noticeable? Was her presence noticeable? Did she love another? Was she loved? Did she have desires? Did she call this punishment or healing? Was this pain greater than the lash? Did she know pleasure? Did they hold each other? Did anyone miss her? Was her absence noticeable? Was her presence noticeable? Did she love another? Was she loved? Did she have desires? Did she call this punishment or healing? Was this pain greater than the lash? Did she know pleasure? Did they hold each other? Did anyone miss her? Was her desire? Was she loved? Was

FISTULA

You were standing at the kitchen counter
preparing a meal for me to eat as you leaked
through your pants. I did not know how to say that you peed
yourself. You did not notice. Your bladder had a mind
of her own, did not seek permission to empty herself.

I pretend not to stare
because you are smiling
because we are alone
because no one else is around to see you wet yourself
because I look up to you
because I would happily keep this secret for you
because this is the only way I know to show love in a world of
     silences
because your private parts have never cried in public before.

KOTEX

When I consider the much-detested stain of the period,
I think not of the monthly sin committed by her continual
    existence
or the evil spirit that must haunt the womb such that her blood
needs to be washed clean and saved by the blood
of Jesus.

I think of the celebration of life when I felt my river flow
again, and again, and again. And as my cup runneth over,
I forgot how I was told that menstruating women could not
enter this place and must worship the god of man
outside of the walls built by man.

I wondered how they would know if a woman chose not to
reveal herself, but then became afraid of what might happen
if the other women would not hold the sacred secret.

When I think of the period rituals, I think not of lips
being discarded or sewn shut to mute the sound of joy,
but of pussy grabbing back and marching down the streets
of cities where children have been born.

They would part the red seas so we could see
into their eyes, eyes seeing red, *blood coming out
of their eyes, or whatever*, a collection
of deviant vajayjays who continue to bleed
so humanity can keep on living.

I think of commercials no longer bleeding blues
when we consider the period.
I think not of shadows and secret hiding places,

but of middle school girls who created their own tongue,
asking the nurse for a "cone" to hold their "ice cream."

They melted in cycles every month.

And because my hips were too narrow,
missing the curves of puberty, I was always upset
that there was never enough of this "ice cream"
for the girls who did not know of Aunt Flo
or when she'd be in town.

When I consider the period, I think of how religions
have always encouraged man
to welcome the visitor.

THE BODY AND OUR RITUALS

So how old were you when it happened?

It was as though this were a conversation about when my first tooth fell out and how we are taught to leave it under our pillows expecting a miracle. There will be an exchange, a compensation, for what has been lost, when the night comes. I close my eyes to dream of the abundance this world will bestow, imagining the fairies watching me for what is now missing, comforted that someone else will know, even if they are just imagined. The day breaks, the sun displaces a moon. I open my eyes and tear the pillow from beneath me, unveiling the bloodstained sheet from the tooth left behind alongside remnants of my girlhood.

It was as though we were sharing stories about the sacred blossoming of bodies and the budding of breasts. How there was a constant ache as flesh stretched beyond the limits of a flat-chested girlhood. This was the sign our youth was over. We now had mountain peaks and the boys would whistle and call to us whenever we walked by switching our narrow hips the way our mothers walked on all the days except for Sunday.

It was as though we were speaking of the menarche and becoming a woman. The first bleed frightened me, how it was Cherry Kool-Aid red; red as though I'd been bruised trying to pop-a-wheelie with the boys; red as though I needed a doctor's touch. But this blood was a different rite of passage also meant to be received with prayers and candles. I turned on the water to fill the tub and lowered myself into the baptism of rose petals and essential oil from the gardenias accompanying the blues that must be soaked in Epsom salt and natural tears. I welcomed in my womanhood, washed in the waters that became blood.

It was as though we were speaking of something wanted; a threshold we knew would be crossed; a place that could never be returned to. All passages change you.

So how old were you when it happened?
I was 16 when I was raped.
Oh, I was 15.

DEAR FATHER,

[page intentionally left blank]

DEAR GYNAECOLOGIST,

I do not remember you touching me during my appointment. Imagine, wanting to be touched. In the beginnings of gynaecology *the practice of examining the female organs was considered repugnant by doctors.* Even your gaze was violation. You crossed your arms, looked through me without looking at me. When you asked why I was taking my supplements, I lied for all good reasons. When you wanted full sentences, I gave you no words. There was something whispering I should rise up off the examination table and run, a resurrection, even with my Black body exposed. Run, until I reached the end. I imagine my body draped in a gown, supine, open. I imagine you holding the knife. I imagine your hands inside of me. I want to crawl inside of myself, escape from your gaze, become my own hiding place. I hold myself because you will not touch me. Your mouth carries too much history, and my atoms remember Mt. Miegs, Alabama.

To be both the subject
and the object of fascination
is not medicine.

WHEN A SCAR GROWS A MOUTH

1. If a woman can earn her stripes when bearing fruit, then am I earned? Do you wear me proudly?
2. Why is what we have been through not called birth? Is it because what has been brought forth is not in your image?
3. What do you bear? What are you bearing? What have you borne?
4. What is boring through you?
5. Are you still an orchard if the fruit they cut from you was not sweet? Or wanted?
6. When they cracked you open, did you know I was summoned to put you back together?
7. Why do you mourn what is evidence of your power?
8. At night, I notice you touch the edges of me. At once gentle, then with trembling hands. You long for a time before me, before my mountain ranges grew across your womb. Are you afraid of me? The way you were afraid of stepping on cracks so you wouldn't break your mother's back? Do you think you are now broken?
9. I am sourced from deep within you.
10. You stood on the sidewalk hypnotized by the root that parted the concrete. It did so to preserve life. Nature already knows *a tree without roots cannot survive the wind*. When will we celebrate that your roots are showing?
11. You try to figure out my chaotic curves. Can you not see I am your Basquiatian crown?
12. I am your masterpiece.
13. Did you know I have given you birth? That I am your second cord?
14. Of life.

DEAR GYNECOLOGIST,

I don't know why I apologized for screaming at you. I didn't mean it, didn't mean to apologize. If my grandmother had been in our examination room, watching you the way I watched you, her bones would have ached from the pressure building beneath the surface— inflammation is a natural response to being worn. She would have smelled that storm in the air, gone in for shelter. *Do you not believe my pain?* What was between us was rank. My mouth an act of God and nature where her catastrophes will come with no remorse. And then the silences; my pounding heart, the fluttering of wings. Enviable and deafening how freedom sounded outside of my body. *No, I do not want to take a seat.* The waters had to break. And after the deluge, I offered you the words I needed most. *I am sorry.* When I was younger, someone stepped on my once white sneakers, and I apologized then too. I wore the blemish of their heavy footprint yet asked them for grace and mercy for taking up room on the sidewalk. After you, I would refuse to go to the doctor for months. After you, I learned to honor the endings. After you, I repented for this world's addiction to Black forgiveness.

The waters had to break. This was my gift to you.

ODE TO MY NECK

Oh, to have a neck that is condemned
for holding my nose so high in the air
that for the first time I know what it is
to breathe.

THE BODY IS NOT A WAR ZONE

If I say I will fight *this*, and *this* is of me
not foreign
not needing permission
but sprouting from me
my own seed
cultivated by my own breath and existence
sourced from within me
part of me
even if it destroys what gives it life.
Me
at the molecular level
me and me and me and me and me and me and me and me and
me and
me and me and me and me and me and me and me and me and
me and me and
me and me and me and me and me and
me and me and me and me and me and me and me and me and
me and
me and me and me and me and me and me and me and me and
me and me and
me and me and
me and me and me and
me and me and me and me and me and me and me and me and
me and me and me and me and me and me and meeeeeeeeeee and
me and me and me and me and
me and me and me and me and me and me and me and me and
me and me and
me and me and me and me and me and me and me and
me unceasingly.
If *this* is me
even when no one understands
where so much of me is coming from
and why so much of me keeps coming
and what to do with me

and how to handle me
and when to plan for me.
Me
who behaves as though I cannot get enough of me
does not know when to quit being me
declares that all of me wants all of me.
If *this* is me
and I say I will fight *this*
then am I fighting   me and   me   and   me
me.

.

I bleed.

Nothin'
but
the
blood.

DEAR GYNECOLOGIST,

Talking to you reminded me of a conversation with a scorned lover, as if this were meant to be an exclusive thing. When you called me I was grocery shopping, had fruit in my basket and a watermelon-sized tumor in my belly. *We need to reschedule your surgery.* I didn't know how to tell you. I have learned to be careful with my *no*, to speak it gently. *But that conflicts with my appointment for a second opinion.* You wanted to know his name. I said I didn't remember. My sovereignty felt hostile, as if I were having an affair with my own body. Like choosing me is a threat. Like your place is dominion. Like knowing I am a trinity of me, myself and I is a failure on your part. A relative once admonished me for not getting along with my mother, wondered why we could not stop having the power struggle that was our relationship. We struggled over this body of mine, her combat zone. This Black body that has no right to herself. This pain body you removed from your surgery schedule because I understood where I begin, and where you end. This body that is learning that this world needs to ask permission. These lessons, never taught by our mothers, or by a world that calls me both Black and woman, and for this I had to be punished. Before you ended the call you asked if I ever felt lightheaded. *Yes. / Well, you are anemic.* And just like that you broke up with me because compassion is a privilege and bodies in pain should know their place.

Talking to you reminded me of a conversation with the lash. I bleed.

LUCY

There was sweat on my brow mixed in with matted hair and the exasperation of continued breath—even though I was ready to meet the maker I was too weary to call for. They press me down until their flesh becomes my flesh and we can no longer tell who is the one being harmed or doing the harming. Black on black on black on black. We are all surviving and dying in the same breath. We share each other in respiration. When I stop breathing, they pound on my breast to call me back into this skin. I cannot escape this flesh. Their hands are skillful in how they simultaneously give life and take it away. They cannot bear being left behind without me—my heart pumps—this is how I am loved. I am home in their arms as they lay me down on the coldness of our surgical table. It is my turn for the knife. We have all been trained well in our bondage. I have nursed for them, today they will nurse for me. They will lie to me. *You will not feel a thing.* Their screams are just as deafening as my own;

Unfasten your legs, ~~he~~ commands
and when they will not part, the women
with condolences on their tongues
open me up to be bruised
in the name of healing
I do not know how to thank them.

We are the dead seas. We gather our woundedness. We witness the suffering of one another. We are each other's cage and comfort. We are forgetting how we wanted to flee, yet, our bodies keep score of the pain until the night. When no one is watching us and I am a crumbled mass of gauze and stitches and crusted over eyes, the women return to me—this time without violence. They embrace me. We weep and give repentance for the sins of our powerlessness. We wipe away what is left of our waters even as we grow afraid of one another with each day. Our nurture is becoming endangered. We hold each other because there is no one else that will hold us. Black on black on black on black. Our seas mix with the salt of our sisters until it runs into each of our inflamed wounds. This too is tenderness.

SHE WHO HAD BEEN DISROBED

Lord
today
I became tired of holding up this world
my arms grew too heavy from carrying this skin
Black
as pain
head heavy with shadowed thoughts
weighed down by locs that refuse to submit
eyes dry from not enough tears
hungry to see beauty in this world
stomach aching for a heavenly feast
free of maggots and lies
breasts hollow from feeding a people
of unrequited love
throat dry from an empty well
screams on deaf ears
desert sands run through my veins
and   my arms
can't muster up the strength
to carry that shield
hold up that sword
hold up this world
I can't afford to fight
yet I can't   prepare to die
Black
as pain
as death
lead-heavy from the weight of this skin

BETSEY

...now for a moment of silence

We who are not meant to be
consumed will hold
our own bodies and blood
delicately in our overflowing
mouths
Sandra Bland
Breonna Taylor
Atatiana Jefferson
Tanesha Anderson
Miriam Carey
Yvette Smith
Aura Rosser
Rekia Boyd
Janisha Fonville
Shereese Francis
Kendra James
Natasha McKenna
Kathryn Johnson
Gabriella Nevarez
Eleanor Bumpers
Tyisha Miller
Mya Hall
Jessica Pettway
Dr. Shalon Irving
Tatia Oden French
Kira Johnson
Tori Bowie
Jahmby Koikai
Aubrion Rogers
Trinity Lillian Graves

We are sisterhood
and bone marrow
where the word unravels
into sinew and teeth
to embrace us all

And now for a moment of silences

Where no one is called
and no thing has happened
here where nothing is remembered
that has not been voiced
the tongues of men
have cut themselves out
in this field of composted flesh
where even the trees have been carefully named
weeping willows pine redwood mahogany
juniper cedar slippery elm basswood teak
black birch cottonwood bamboo acacia
black oak sugar maple common ash
black ash baobab eucalyptus sequoia
black willow beech black walnut
black locust black hickory

And now for the moment of silences

Blood of our blood
that stings wherever it runs
because they have only wept

when the mother is an earth
that has ravaged what is cherished
we multi-tongued women
whose bodies are abandoned houses
with dominion over the nothing
and everything
we are not called

in order to disremember
what cannot be forgotten
this lineage of destruction
this ritual of ending the stillness in
waters that carry the names of storms
Katrina Lili Opal Rita Irene
Sandy Isabel Iris Roxanne
Wilma Joan Alicia Fran Gloria
Diana Allison Ingrid Jeanne Frances
Irma Florence Erika Maria
were feared for their fury
and called themselves into existence
to remind us of a force so consuming
that their names can never be used
again for the hurricanes that
will keep on coming

And now for the moment of silence

That swallowed up little Black girls
from a Secondary School in 2014
by ~~Boko Haram~~
as currency
of bodies to be used
over 1,000 girls since 2013
on the altars of men

and wars that continue
to call itself power in its own
name boasts how many little
Black girls *Stolen Girls* in 1963 Americus
Georgia can be imprisoned without
charges without parents knowing
because their daughters spoke

in ways they could not protested
they too had had enough
and stood in line for tickets
to integrate a movie theater
We did not move
Sandra Russell
Lulu M. Westbrook
Willie Mae Smith
Emma Jean Jones
Vyrtis Jackson
Evette Hose
Verna Hollis
Shirley Ann Green
Agnes Carter
Gloria Breedlove
Gloria Dean
Pearl Brown
Diane Dorsey
Henrietta   Fuller
Juanita Freeman
huddled in jail cells where their legs
were too short to touch the ground
that is full and fat with the Black
& Missing children in 2019
since silence has always been
the weapon of choice

But now for a moment

Betsey
on a surgical table
with legs spread eagle
to give him unlimited
access to her body swollen
from infection of unsterilized
silk and gut sutures stitched into
her with only the women as witness
black on black on black on black
Betsey
on a surgical table
with legs spread eagle
her dried blood the color of
black on black on black on black
to declare she has now been
cured with the silver sutures
entangled in her
closed womb
in the cold sterility
of how we have learned
to tell these stories
Betsey
on a surgical table
black
on black
on black
on black
everywhere open
reaching   reaching   reaching
for her own salvation

Say. her. name.

THE RIVER FLOWS WITHOUT WAITING

She said I had the hands
of homeopathy,

like my hands have made her
remedies. Medicine

woman. Maker of soups
with ginger root, balms for

many souls traversing
waters, insatiable

currents, like the laying
on of hands. Medicine

woman's hands, the tonic
for our perishing.

ANARCHA

I have come into this world a call to arms. Black on black on black on black and roots made bare. Do not mind the ways in which we consume the earth in our unmarked graves, forever connected to her cycles so the calla lilies always return to the place where my birth mother's blood mixed with the dirt. Everywhere her waters were breaking. Do not mind the ways in which we flood, or the ways in which this world will drown in us. We are forever—a deluge, calla lilies always resurrecting, unceasing in how we exist; how we haunt every season when we bloom where we are planted and fertilized the soil with our marrow. We bloom cacophonously; we were never meant to be tamed. Black on black on black on black, and I cannot tell myself apart from them all with their crimson petals. We are a woman possessed with our own bodies and the wind carries our complicated scent. Do not mind the ways in which you suffocate, smoldering in our discarded silence. There will be no more sacrificial offerings on these altars because endings are as primal and as necessary as the new moon.

To the nescient eye, blood looks black at night. Black on black on black on black, she was coming undone. Separated. Separated. Separated. It was unsightly how she tore away at the earth until the roots were reaching back for her. She cracked open and I dared to come out of my mother's womb covered in the blood of all that could not be eroded from our memory. The only power she knew was how to give birth. And how to name. Anarchist. That was enough.

The bodies
The bodies
The bodies
The bodies
The bodies
The bodies
The bodies
The bodies
The bodies
The bodies
The bodies
The bodies
The bodies
The bodies
The bodies
The bodies
The bodies
The bodies
The bodies
The bodies
The bodies
The bodies
The bodies
The bodies
The bodies
The bodies
The bodies
The bodies
The bodies
The bodies
The bodies
The bodies
The bodies
The bodies
The bodies
The bodies
The bodies
The bodies
The bodies
The bodies
The bodies
The bodies
The bodies
The bodies
The bodies

I bleed.

THE BODIES. IN PAIN.

Something terrible happened here.

Keeps happening here because a ~~people~~ ~~nation~~ narrative developed a taste for our blood and our milk mixed with the salt of our tears, how the body tears, bodies pressed against bodies pressed against bodies pressed against bodies pressed against bodies so more Black bodies could be born   into this. Is this what is meant by being born in sin, shapen in iniquity? And we kept being born   into this. The lives that came through us was more resilience than miracle as whyte women lamented that *continuously having children and continuously nursing her* own *children made her 'a slave'* so she made sure we kept being born   into this. I wonder how much of our pain was in our milk? Black bellies fat with babies that bore the complexion of violence because studies have confirmed that pregnancy is contagious. So is brutality.

Something terrible happened here.

Keeps happening here though the Black bodies trafficked across the trans-Saharan routes for the other racial slavery were not wanted in all the same ways, so our men were castrated. Mating season has its brutalities. I am not sure which is worse, to be born   into this after the Atlantic, or to be deprived of being born after the Sahara. I wonder why I am compelled to measure one against the other for degrees of brutality. How the measuring itself is brutal. How the not measuring is brutal. How the trans-Atlantic genocides lasted over four centuries, and the Saharan lasted seventeen. How the women were preferred to men, were taken at triple the rate, are still being taken. How there is no way to ever know how many Black bodies were scattered. How the not knowing is brutal. How the knowing is brutal. How closing the Atlantic borders did not end the commodification / persecution / abduction / harvesting / pillaging / poaching of Black bodies from Africa. How commercial language has no place here. How the figures lose their value. How the word *slave* took on new meanings. How systems of antiquity have ways of preserving themselves. How forgetting has a cost. How remembering has a cost.

Something terrible happens here.

Keeps happening here even though ~~General Robert E. Lee~~ warned about memorializing in this way because it would only keep open the sores of war. Still, after their war was lost, they built over 700 ~~statues~~ altars because some bodies are always to be mourned and some bodies are unmournable. The wyte women— raised on our milk—were *instrumental in raising funds* to commemorate the brutalities of their men; held bake sales of sweet pastries that leave an aftertaste. The sores were everywhere; it is the nature of illness to spread in this way. ~~James Marion Sims~~ alone was in Alabama, Philadelphia, South Carolina, and New York with its bronze edifice known for its resistance to corrosion. The fibroid tumors often return if malignant conditions are not addressed. When my new doctor asks if there are any illnesses they should know of, I tell them America is my pre-existing condition. Recent research to explain the health vulnerabilities of being Black in America shows the more time spent in the U.S. is the greatest predictor for health decline, even for a foreign-born Black person. *The stress of racism may be particularly virulent and pathogenic. Monuments are not intended for the dead* but for the dying.

Something terrible happens here.

Keeps happening here every time the word *slave* is used as a noun *person, place, thing, or idea*; instead of the adjective *enslaved* that *modifies or limits the noun.* This is more than semantics; this is the language of conquest spoken by a world that has never imagined some bodies as free. How unimaginative that prosperity must come from wounded Black bodies rather than from miracle. *What God do you serve?* ~~Slave~~ was not always synonymous with Blackness, but as demand for enslaved bodies grew, so did racism. Yteness was not always synonymous with ~~Master, owner,~~ or ~~purchaser~~ of bodies created to be loved, but enslavers and violators who were never sanctioned by divine authority. *What God do you serve?* How language ~~preserves~~ creates structures of power where Black bodies / people / humans / prisoners of wars / unwilling immigrants were chained and then named ~~slave~~. And by whom? How language is a necessary component of violence so even ~~if~~ when Black bodies ran free, they were diagnosed with *drapetomania, the disease causing negroes to run away.* Some psychologists now say speech can be violence and *a culture of constant, casual brutality is toxic to the body, and we suffer for it.* As if   I haven't already been emptied of my tears.

Something terrible is happening here.

Keeps happening here in a body not yet fully free. Pressed my wet palm against my breast to feel life still cycling through me. *Take a deep breath.* This is the consecration. *Open your mouth.* Your names are on our tongues Anarcha, Lucy, Betsey and all those unnamed in Mt. Meigs, Alabama. We call out to the other Mothers of Gynecology in Prince Edward County, Virginia (1837). And the unnamed Mothers of Ovariotomy in Danville, Kentucky. And the unnamed Mothers of the C-section in Haiti before their revolution, then Donaldsonville, Louisiana. And the unnamed mothers whose wombs were used as bondage on the waters of the Atlantic. And the unnamed mothers who are a part of the Sahara. And the unnamed mothers who were forced across the Red Sea. And the unnamed who were never mothered in the unnamed places. Like ritual, we build you an altar Anarcha and pour libations at your feet. *The young woman known as Anarcha, was erected in protest only to be stolen in the night.* Like ritual, we call in the rains. We salt, we kin and with winds over 150 mph Hurricane Laura made a casualty out of a ~~statue~~ in Louisiana because ~~confederate~~ means joined by agreement. Like ritual, we bleed and let the monumental reckonings be washed in the blood memory. Though science *assumed* we wouldn't remember, recent studies show a *mother's epigenetic memory is essential for the development and survival of the new generation.* Like ritual, we keep being born. Violence has happened here. *They'll be reborn. We want to welcome them back to Montgomery but this time to be handled with care.*

There's a difference between remembrance of history and reverence of it.

Something terrible happened here.

Keeps happening here. There is no cure for this. No metaphor for this. No other way to say this.

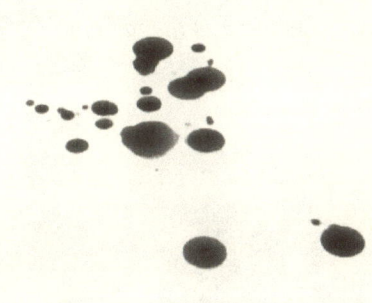

I bleed
and do not die.

"If we were made for nothing else, we were made to heal."

- Lucille Clifton

ACKNOWLEDGMENTS

I give thanks to the ancestors who trusted me with the stories of our bodies, and the ancestors whose stories have yet to be told. I am especially grateful for your encouragement to remain in the world of the living while my body was convalescing. To my body, thank you for continued breath.

To my younger sister, Christina E. Campbell, thank you for always loving from the moment you were born. The way you have always valued my stories has saved me so often from the perils of doubt. Thank you to my bonus grandmother, Mommy Ida, for loving me in ways that didn't hurt; to my mother for being my first teacher on the complex nature of the wound; and to my collective mothers and sisters for being my village even when I didn't know how to receive.

To the faculty at Columbia's Writing MFA program, thank you, Keri Bertino, for noticing I needed support even before I noticed; Joseph Fasano for encouraging me to write my obsession; the late Richard Howard for unexpectedly reading my pap smear poem aloud to everyone with such wonder I started to love myself more (after I recovered from my quiet embarrassment); Bill Wadsworth for your groundedness when I couldn't find my footing; Laila Maher for being the Dean and my friend; Aracelis Girmay for holding me when I cried in your arms on my first day back to Columbia post-surgery, you felt like grade school, warm milk, and a prayer; Timothy Donnelly for curating an Independent Study on writing trauma to support my return to the page; and Lynn Melnick for being my Advisor through the tumult of stories flowing through me. Thank you to everyone who wrote reference letters, encouraged me to keep breathing and writing, workshopped with me, or shared opportunities. Thank you to my Narrative Medicine colleagues for being friends even after I lovingly stalked the *Illness and Disabilities Narrative* course until I could enroll. In this space, I learned to not turn away from the stories our bodies tell.

Thank you to the following platforms for publishing some of the stories in this book: TEDx Talk, The Poetry Foundation, *The Amistad Literary Arts Journal*, *Intima: A Journal of Narrative Medicine*, and The Edinburgh Festival Fringe through the loving encouragement of Nicole Ansari-Cox and Producer Brian Cox. Thank you to the Café Royal Cultural Foundation for a literary grant in support of my work, the Twenty Summers Residency, and the BLKSPACE Residency for a space to rest from telling our stories.

Thank you, Amy Bishop, for being such an attuned literary agent that you honored my manuscript in a way that felt more like honoring my individual and ancestral body. In your presence, my agency always had room to breathe. Thank you, Jodie Toohey, for your commitment, generosity, and support throughout the publishing process. Thank you Theik Smith for reflecting my embodied stories through the art of photography. Thank you to my Black female therapists because self-care looks good on everyone.

Deepest gratitude to all who supported this journey through donations, encouragement, and unwavering belief in the importance of voice. Your contributions, both tangible and intangible, have been instrumental in bringing UNRULY to life.

Thank you, readers, for accompanying me/us on the embodied journey through UNRULY.

And thank you to myself because self-love is medicine.

IMAGES

Fig. 1
Date: August 19, 2017
Credit: Eduardo Munoz, Reuters Pictures
Women paint their clothes with red as they take part in protest against white supremacy.
Note: The image has been modified with a censor bar over the eyes of the statue.

Fig. 2
Caption: This hospitalized neonate was displaying a bodily rigidity produced by Clostridium tetani exotoxin. This condition is known as neonatal tetanus.
Date: January 1, 1995
Credit: Centers for Disease Control and Prevention's Public Health Image Library
Source: https://phil.cdc.gov/details.aspx?pid=6374

Fig. 3
Cobbler's Stabbing Awl
Credit: Comugnero Silvana
Source: Adobe Stock

Fig. 4
Tongue Restraint
Source: Institute of Jamaica

Fig. 5
Credit: Theik Smith Photography

Model: Antoinette Cooper

Fig. 6
Credit: Theik Smith Photography
Model: Antoinette Cooper

Fig. 7
Date: August 27, 2020
Credit: Mickey Welsh, USA TODAY NETWORK via Imagn Content Services, LLC
Hurricane Laura toppled a confederate statue that withstood earlier protests in Lake Charles, LA.
Note: The image has been modified with a censor bar over the eyes of the statue.

Fig. 8
Date: August 29, 2015
Credit: NYstudio
Source: iStock by Getty Images

WORKS REFERENCED

Adeyi, Moradeyo. "10 Black Men Share Why They Love Black Women." *MadameNoire*, 30 Mar. 2020, madamenoire. com/1100383/10-black-men-share-why-they-love-black-women.

Balingit, Moriah. "A Gynecologist Secretly Photographed Patients. What's Their Pain Worth?" *Washington Post*, 14 Jan 2017, www.washingtonpost.com/local/education/a-gynecologist-secretly-photographed-patients-whats-their-pain-worth/2017/01/14/35bcf156-d45e-11e6-a783-cd3fa950f2fd_story.html.

Barrett, Lisa Feldman. "Opinion | When Is Speech Violence?" *The New York Times*, 14 July 2017, www.nytimes.com/2017/07/14/opinion/sunday/when-is-speech-violence.html.

Bellamy, Claretta. "What Black Women Should Know About Hair Relaxers and Their Health." *NBC News*, 18 Oct. 2023, www.nbcnews.com/news/nbcblk/black-women-hair-relaxers-cancer-rcna117685.

Bishop, Rudine Sims. "Mirrors, Windows, and Sliding Glass Doors." *Perspectives: Choosing and Using Books for the Classroom*, vol. 6, no. 3, Summer 1990, ix-xi.

Blaisdell, Aaron P, et al. "From Heart Beats to Health Recipes: The Role of Fractal Physiology in the Ancestral Health Movement." *Journal of Evolution and Health*, vol. 1, no. 1, 4 Dec. 2013, https://doi.org/10.15310/2334-3591.1001.

Blankenship, Bradley George Grant. "The Girls of the Leesburg Stockade." *Georgia Public Broadcasting*, 14 Aug. 2020, www.gpb.org/news/2016/08/15/the-girls-of-the-leesburg-stockade.

Closson, Hailey. "Deep in the Woods, an Incredible Story Behind a Former Enslaved Woman's Grave." *CNS Maryland*, 4 Apr. 2024, https://cnsmaryland.org/2024/04/04/deep-in-the-woods-an-incredible-story-behind-a-former-enslaved-womans-grave/.

Doamekpor, Lauren A., and Gniesha Y. Dinwiddie. "Allostatic Load in Foreign-Born and US-Born Blacks: Evidence from the 2001–2010 National Health and Nutrition Examination Survey." *American Journal of Public Health*, vol. 105, no. 3, Mar. 2015, pp. 591–597, https://doi.org/10.2105/ajph.2014.302285.

Fenton, Justin. "Suspicious Co-worker Tipped Johns Hopkins in Levy Case." *Baltimore Sun*, 1 June 2019, www.baltimoresun.com/2014/08/29/suspicious-co-worker-tipped-johns-hopkins-in-levy-case-2.

Gakunzi, David. "The Arab-Muslim Slave Trade: Lifting the Taboo." *Jewish Political Studies Review*, vol. 29, no. 3/4, 2018, pp. 40–42, www.jstor.org/stable/26500685.

Green, Erica L., and Justin Fenton. "Hopkins Settlement Not the End for Victims." *Baltimore Sun*, 29 June 2019, www.baltimoresun.com/2014/07/22/hopkins-settlement-not-the-end-for-victims.

Hallman J. C. "J. Marion Sims and the Civil War — a Rollicking Tale of Deceit and Spycraft." *Montgomery Advertiser*, 29 Sept. 2018, www.montgomeryadvertiser.com/story/opinion/2018/09/28/dr-j-marion-sims-and-civil-war-rollicking-tale-deceit-and-spycraft-slaves-experiments/1443452002.

Hallman, J. C. "Monumental Error." *Harper's Magazine*, Nov. 2017, harpers.org/archive/2017/11/monumental-error.

Harmon, Quaker E., et al. "Keloids and Ultrasound Detected Fibroids in Young African American Women." *PLoS ONE*, vol. 8, no. 12, 27 Dec. 2013, p. e84737, https://doi.org/10.1371/journal.pone.0084737.

Hoffman, Kelly M., et al. "Racial Bias in Pain Assessment and Treatment Recommendations, and False Beliefs about Biological Differences between Blacks and Whites." *Proceedings of the National Academy of Sciences*, vol. 113, no. 16, 2016, pp. 4296–4301, doi:10.1073/pnas.1516047113.

Holland, Brynn. "The "Father of Modern Gynecology" Performed Shocking Experiments on Slaves." *History.com*, History, 4 Dec. 2018, www.history.com/news/the-father-of-modern-gynecology-performed-shocking-experiments-on-slaves.

Hughes, Langston. "Mother to Son." *The Crisis*, vol. 25, no. 2, Dec. 1922, p. 87

Hughes, Virginia. "Mice Inherit the Fears of Their Fathers." *Science*, 15 Nov. 2013, www.nationalgeographic.com/science/article/mice-inherit-the-fears-of-their-fathers.

Jackson, Gabrielle. ""Disgusting" Study Rating Attractiveness of Women with Endometriosis Retracted by Medical Journal." *The Guardian*, 5 Aug. 2020, www.theguardian.com/society/2020/aug/05/disgusting-study-rating-attractiveness-of-women-with-endometriosis-retracted-by-medical-journal.

Jones-Rogers, Stephanie E. *They Were Her Property: White Women as Slave Owners in the American South*. New Haven, Yale University Press, 2019.

Landrieu, Mitch. "Mitch Landrieu Takes History off a Pedestal." *Lapham's Quarterly*, 19 May 2017, www.laphamsquarterly.org/memory/mitch-landrieu-takes-history-pedestal.

Lewis, Gabrielle, Victoria Ifatusin, and Jamille Whitlow. "A Pregnant Woman's Lynching Resonates Through the Generations." *Capital News Service*, 17 Nov. 2021, https://lynching.cnsmaryland.org/2021/11/10/mary-turner-lynching-georgia/.

Lindsey, Treva. "The Urgent Crisis of Missing Black Women and Girls." *Women's Media Center*, 20 Feb. 2020, www.womensmediacenter.com/news-features/the-urgent-crisis-of-missing-black-women-and-girls.

Little, Becky. "How the US Got So Many Confederate Monuments." *HISTORY*, 8 Sept. 2021, www.history.com/news/how-the-u-s-got-so-many-confederate-monuments.

Loevy, Katharine. "Literary Resistance to the Philosophy of Slavery: Al-Farabi and the Ikhwan Al-Safa'." *Philosophy and Literature*, vol. 44, no. 2, 2020, pp. 237–254, https://doi.org/10.1353/phl.2020.0020.

Max-Planck-Gesellschaft. "Epigenetics between the generations: We inherit more than just genes." *ScienceDaily*, 17 July 2017, www.sciencedaily.com/releases/2017/07/170717100548.htm.

(Note: In 1997, the Max Planck Society appointed a committee of independent historians to comprehensively address the inhumane history of its predecessor organization, www.mpg.de/history/kws-under-national-socialism.)

"Memorialization of Robert E. Lee and the Lost Cause - Arlington House, the Robert E. Lee Memorial (U.S. National Park Service)." *www.nps.gov*, 14 Sept. 2021, www.nps.gov/arho/learn/historyculture/memorialization-of-robert-e-lee-and-the-lost-cause.htm.

"More than 1,000 Children in Northeastern Nigeria Abducted by Boko Haram since 2013." *www.unicef.org*, 13 Apr. 2018, www.unicef.org/press-releases/more-than-1000-children-northeastern-nigeria-abducted-boko-haram-since-2013.

Ojanuga, Durrenda. "The Medical Ethics of the "Father of Gynaecology", Dr J Marion Sims." *Journal of Medical Ethics*, vol. 19, no. 1, 1 Mar. 1993, pp. 28–31, jme.bmj.com/content/medethics/19/1/28.full.pdf, https://doi.org/10.1136/jme.19.1.28.

Owens, Deirdre Cooper. *Medical Bondage : Race, Gender, and the Origins of American Gynecology*. University Of Georgia Press, 2017.

Owens, Deirdre Cooper, and Sharla M. Fett. "Black Maternal and Infant Health: Historical Legacies of Slavery." *American Journal of Public Health*, vol. 109, no. 10, Oct. 2019, pp. 1342–1345, ajph.aphapublications.org/doi/full/10.2105/AJPH.2019.305243, https://doi.org/10.2105/ajph.2019.305243.

Philips, John Edward. "Some Recent Thinking on Slavery in Islamic Africa and the Middle East." *Middle East Studies Association Bulletin*, vol. 27, no. 2, 1993, pp. 157–162, www.jstor.org/stable/23061313.

Vankin, Deborah. "Monument Honors Enslaved Women's Role in History of Gynecology - Los Angeles Times." *Los Angeles Times*, 6 Mar. 2021, www.latimes.com/entertainment-arts/story/2021-03-05/mothers-of-gynecology-j-marion-sims.

Vercellini, Paolo, et al. "RETRACTED: Attractiveness of Women with Rectovaginal Endometriosis: A Case-Control Study." *Fertility and Sterility*, vol. 99, no. 1, Jan. 2013, pp. 212–218, https://doi.org/10.1016/j.fertnstert.2012.08.039.

"What Not to Say to Dr. Levy's and Johns Hopkins Hospital's Victims." *Schochor, Staton, Goldberg and Cardea, P.A.*, 5 Mar. 2013, sfspa.com/not-say-dr-levys-johns-hopkins-hospitals-victims.

Yehuda, Rachel, and Amy Lehrner. "Intergenerational Transmission of Trauma Effects: Putative Role of Epigenetic Mechanisms." *World Psychiatry*, vol. 17, no. 3, 2018, pp. 243–257, www.ncbi.nlm.nih.gov/pmc/articles/PMC6127768/, https://doi.org/10.1002/wps.20568.

The Nyame Dua, or "tree of God," represents the presence of the divine in nature and in our lives. It is a symbol of protection and a sacred space where rituals are performed, reminding us of the spiritual dimension of our collective healing journey.